*Y*our birthday is so important to me,
I could fill a book with my feelings.

To:

From:

Date:

THE
Too-Bad-It's-Your-Birthday
BOOK

THE
Too-Bad-It's-Your-Birthday
BOOK

Tender Thoughts to Put a Smile on Your Wrinkly Little Face

James Dale

S T A R K
B O O K S
an Andrews McMeel
Publishing Imprint

The Too-Bad-It's-Your-Birthday Book copyright © 2000 by James Dale.
All rights reserved. Printed in China. No part of this book may be used or repro-
duced in any manner whatsoever without written permission except in the case of
reprints in the context of reviews. For information, write Andrews McMeel
Publishing, an Andrews McMeel Universal company,
4520 Main Street, Kansas City, Missouri 64111.

00 01 02 03 04 RDC 10 9 8 7 6 5 4 3 2 1

Library of Congress Cataloging-in-Publication Data
Dale, Jim, 1948–
   The too-bad-it's-your-birthday book : a few tender thoughts to put a smile on
your wrinkly little face / by James Dale.
      p. cm.
   ISBN 0-7407-1087-7
      1. Aging—Humor. 2. Birthdays—Humor. I. Title.
PN6231.A43 D35 2000
818'.5402—dc21   00-31049
                  Book design by Holly Camerlinck

Attention: Schools and Businesses

Andrews McMeel books are available at quantity discounts with bulk purchase
for educational, business, or sales promotional use. For information, please write to:
Special Sales Department, Andrews McMeel Publishing, 4520 Main Street,
Kansas City, Missouri 64111.

*S*o you're having another birthday.

That's a tragic pity
with no redeeming aspects.

*L*ife is like a bowl of cereal.

And these are the soggy years.

*B*irthday after birthday, boys always fought over you.

Me, they tossed a coin for.

A Birthday Fantasy:

A great-looking guy waiting on you hand and foot.

Hey, I warned you it was a fantasy.

*L*ove your birthday.
Love the celebration.
Love you.

Hate how young you look.

Remember, guys swear, smoke, gamble, and drink.

And we women pretty much run the world.

You know, nothing in the world is more important
to me than your birthday . . .

. . . unless my phone rings.

These days, they say you can recycle anything.

Hey, let's be virgins again.

*B*elieve me, fat isn't all bad.

It stretches out the wrinkles.

A Birthday Thought:

Some women don't wear makeup and still look good.

There should be a special tax on them.

*W*ow! You don't need plastic surgery.

Or you've already had it and it was so good,
nobody can tell.

If you're like me, you're attracted to smart men . . .

. . . who are naked.

*B*irthday girl, we grew up together.

Well, one of us grew up.

*Y*ou really understand me . . .

. . . and even I don't understand me.

Remember when we were kids and we hunted fossils?

And now we're what we hunted for.

On your birthday, every minute I spend without you
is agony . . .

. . . except Thursday nights when there's really
good stuff on TV.

*D*on't get down about getting older.

Some wart-covered lizards live to be over two hundred.
(But nobody wants to touch them.)

You know what's great about celebrating your birthday by watching TV?

You don't have to go anywhere.

*Y*ou aren't the type to make a birthday wish for one of those muscular beefcake guys.

Unless it's just for the day.

*M*en gather around you like . . .

. . . men.

On your birthday, someone who cares about you will make dinner . . .

. . . reservations.

*I*n the World Wide Web of life . . .

. . . you're always welcome at my home page.

Girl-to-Girl Birthday Question:

*I*f you're thinking of celebrating by having cybersex . . .

. . . who gets on top, you or the computer?

*L*et's celebrate your birthday the way they did
in the Szechuan province during the Ming dynasty.

We'll pick up Chinese food.

This may sound bitchy but . . .

*N*ever looking any older is getting on everyone's nerves.

This may sound bitchy but . . .

Get some wrinkles!

This may sound bitchy but . . .

Your figure could stand some cellulite!

This may sound bitchy but . . .

Eating whatever you want and never gaining weight isn't winning you a lot of friends.

*S*ome people believe if you get kissed on your birthday, you turn into a princess.

Worst case, at least you got kissed.

Birthday Test:

- Does it seem like newspapers and books are printed in smaller type each year?
- Do you believe the freedom to complain should be in the Bill of Rights?
- Are you in favor of a tax on people younger than you?

On your birthday, I'm not going to make any more insulting comments about your age.

It wouldn't be nice to make fun of a decrepit, senile biddy like you.

I don't want to sound like an old grouch but . . .

Why do people pierce their tongues?

I don't want to sound like an old grouch but . . .

Don't you think women with tattoos are usually sluts?

I don't want to sound like an old grouch but . . .

What's with everybody exercising all the time?

I don't want to sound like an old grouch but . . .

What's the good part about Madonna?

Was it Patrick Henry's wife who said on her birthday:

"Give me something expensive or give me
nothing at all?"

Here's a Fun Birthday Game:

1. Write down your age   _____
2. Subtract 10   _-10_
3. Imagine that's your age   _____

Okay, game's over, add the 10 back.

*R*emember when you were a kid
and you stayed in the bathtub and got all wrinkly?

Guess you stayed too long?

Scientists now have a theory on why you feel bad on your birthday.

You're very old.

*S*o, it's your birthday. Things could be worse.

It could be your birthday and you could clean public bathrooms for a living.

I wouldn't betray your real age
for all the money in the world.

But for two extra-strength Advil when I have
a killer headache, I'd spill everything.

Now that you're older, you can admit it.

You watch the Weather Channel.

*H*ey, even at our age, we're still swingers.

But now when we swing,
we get dizzy and have hot flashes.

An International Birthday Message:

*A*s ze French say, you're très old.

*F*or your birthday, I wanted to get you a strand of giant deep-sea pearls, so, first, I recruited a team of trained diving snails. The snails creep along the shore, trudge into the salty ocean, and plod their way to the darkest depths of the sea. There, the snails search out the rarest clams, pry them open, one after another, until they find one flawless giant pearl. Then, the snails carefully roll it back to shallow water, nudge the pearl to the shore, all the way to me. Then, they trudge back into the brine, find another rare clam, pry it open in search of another flawless pearl, over and over, pearl after pearl, until they finally assemble enough for a strand.

So . . . now it's just a matter of waiting for the snails.

Birthday girl, you're so mature.

You must be *way* older than me.

A Birthday Thought That's Not Politically Correct:

What's so wrong with skinning the fur off of rodents
to make winter coats?

A Birthday Thought That's Not Politically Correct:

Couldn't we just get a mild case of anorexia?

A Birthday Thought That's Not Politically Correct:

Do we really want to have compost heaps?

A Birthday Thought That's Not Politically Correct:

What's so wrong with marrying somebody really rich?

If you lie on your back and stare at the ceiling,
pretty soon the whole room seems like it's upside down.

(When we get older, it doesn't take much
to entertain us.)

*H*onest . . . *ha-ha* . . . *hee-hee* . . .

You still look young . . . HA-HA-HA!

I have your actual age written on a piece of paper . . .

. . . so don't piss me off!

*Y*our friends got together to light all your birthday candles.

Oops, not enough friends.

*C*ondolences on your birthday.

I'm sorry to hear your youth has passed away.

Sometimes your hearing goes as you get older.

SOMETIMES
IT'S
YOUR
EYES.

Vacuuming sucks.

But birthdays aren't far behind.

*I*t's your birthday.

Okay, enough about you, mine's next.